*To Elaine, Lucy and William,*
*with love - T.M.*

ORCHARD BOOKS
96 Leonard Street, London EC2A 4XD
*Orchard Books Australia*
14 Mars Road, Lane Cove, NSW 2066
First published in Great Britain in 1998
First paperback publication 1999
Text © Tony Mitton 1998
Illustrations © Martin Chatterton 1998
The rights of Tony Mitton to be identified as the author
and Martin Chatterton as the illustrator of this work have been
asserted by them in accordance with the Copyright,
Designs and Patents Act, 1988.
A CIP catalogue record for this book is available
from the British Library.
1 86039 691 7 (hardback)
1 86039 882 0 (paperback)
Printed in Great Britain.

# Tony Mitton

# MONSTER RAPS

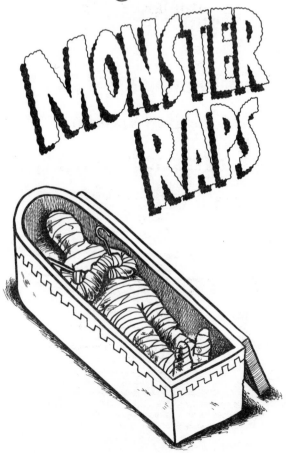

## illustrated by Martin Chatterton

 ORCHARD BOOKS

Try reading Royal Raps, Big Bad Raps or Fangtastic Raps next, or I'll tell my Mummy

there lived a king
in Egypt's land -
you know, that place
with piles of sand.
Tut-an-kha-mun
was his name...
I can't pronounce it,
what a shame!

I'll have to give
that name the boot
and call him, just for short,
King Toot.

Now this old king
we're calling Toot,
had a great big palace
with lots of loot,
and faithful servants
dressed with taste,
with neat, bobbed hair
and towels round the waist.

Now King Toot's gang
told everyone
that their king shone
like the midday sun.
But the gang all knew it,
yup, you bet:
every sun
is bound to set.

GULP!

OK, I'll say it
plain and dry:
even a king
has got to die.

So King Toot stood
by the banks of the Nile.
"Alright," he said.
"Let's do it in style.

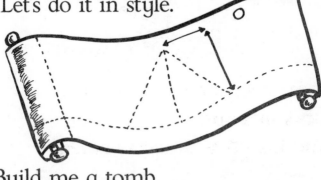

Build me a tomb,
and build it grand,
so it rises high
from the desert sand.
And fill it full
of food and treasure,
'cos after death
I'm planning pleasure.
(I hear that heaven's
a land of leisure.)"

So his men brought massive
rocks in ships.
And his slaves, they sweated
under whips.

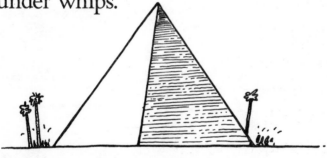

Well, soon that tomb,
it towered up high,
square at the base
with a point in the sky.

And the head priest said,
"OK, that's it.
We hope your tomb's
a tidy fit."
King Toot said, "Yup,
that'll do the trick.
Now, I'll just lie down
for I'm feeling sick.

It must have been
that funny drink.
I wish I'd poured it
down the sink."

32

He went to sleep
on the royal bed,
and before too long
King Toot lay dead.
But no one flapped
and no one fussed,
for King Toot's servants
had it sussed.

They wrapped him up,
like the head priest said,
with bandages
from foot to head,
till he lay there looking
nice and neat,
completely wrapped
from head to feet.

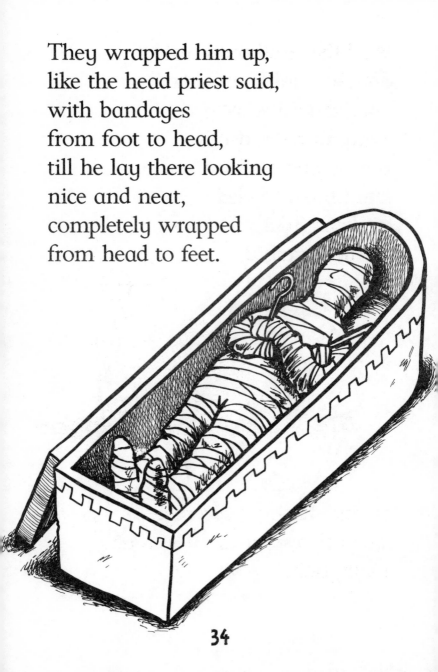

And the head priest said,
"Right. That's enough.
Now put him in
with all his stuff."
So they painted his coffin
and closed the lid
and put the lot
in the pyramid.

And they came on out,
saying, "Toot, night-night."
Then they shut that tomb up
really tight.

So King Toot slept
for a thousand years,
which is when our hero,
Mort, appears.

Now Mort was quick,
yes, Mort was fast,
and Mort liked digging
up the past.
An important fact,
not to be missed:
Mort was an
archaeologist.
(And the pyramid
was on his list.)

So Mort got busy
and soon undid
the door to King Toot's
pyramid.
He went down the tunnel
that led to the room
deep in the heart
of the royal tomb.

He took one look
and he called out, "Wow!
I'm made," he said,
"I'm famous now.

I'll put these things
where folk can see 'em,
under glass
in a big museum."

**"OH, NO, YOU WON'T,"**
a deep voice said.
It seemed to come
from King Toot's head.

"Say," said Mort,
"it's a mummy case
with a real neat pic
of King Toot's face!"

The lid flew open.
Up sat Toot.

"Hey!" cried Mort,
"I love the suit.
In all my days
I've never seen
a corpse look quite
so neat and clean."

40

But the mummy boomed out,
"So, you choose
to interrupt
the royal snooze.
This is the tomb
of an ancient king.
You didn't knock.
You didn't ring.

So watch things turn
from bad to worse.
Now hear me cast
the Mummy's Curse!"

"Wait!" cried Mort.
"You've got it wrong.

Now listen to me.
We ain't got long.
There are tourists coming
any day now.
They'll barge in here
and make a row.
The plane is booked.
They'll soon be here,
with cameras flashing
and cans of beer.

It's the Pyramid Package
with a camel ride.
They'll visit your tomb
and tramp inside.
If you don't believe me,
ask the Sphinx.
They'll soon see off
your forty winks.

So don't just lie here
looking pretty.
Come with me
to London City.

I'll take you there
with all your stuff.
And if you think
that ain't enough,
there are cases there
with soundproof glass.
You can lie in peace
while people pass.

And everyone
will know your name.
How about that, then -
Peace and Fame!"

"Mmm," boomed Toot,
"well, that sounds great."
So Mort brought in
a monstrous crate.

And carefully
he packed King Toot,
with his fancy coffin
and all his loot,
saying, "See you soon, King.
Have a nice ride.
I'll get you out
at the other side."

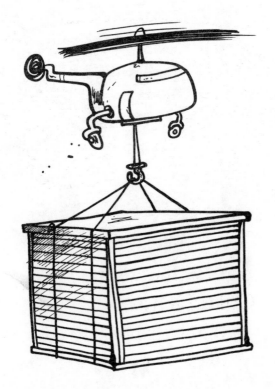

And when he did,
old Toot was glad.
He boomed, "Hey, this
is a real nice pad.
I'll take that case there
by the door."
Then he clambered in
and began to snore.

And he slept in peace,
with royal ease,
for a sign on the wall
said, 'Quiet Please'.

Now Toot is famous.
Mort is too.
So come on folks,
come down and view
the ancient treasure
of Old King Toot,
with his mummy case
and his bandage suit
and his silver spoon
and his golden cup,

'cos here's the end.
That wraps it up.

# CONTENTS

**O**nce upon a time,
in a town on the Rhine,
lived a guy by the name of
Frankenstein.

Now, Frankenstein
was a bit of a boff.
There wasn't a thing
he couldn't pull off.
So Frank said it
was his intention
to amaze the world
with a great invention.

But he couldn't decide
just what it should be,
so he bruised his brain,
saying, "Let me see...

How about a ship
that sails through space?

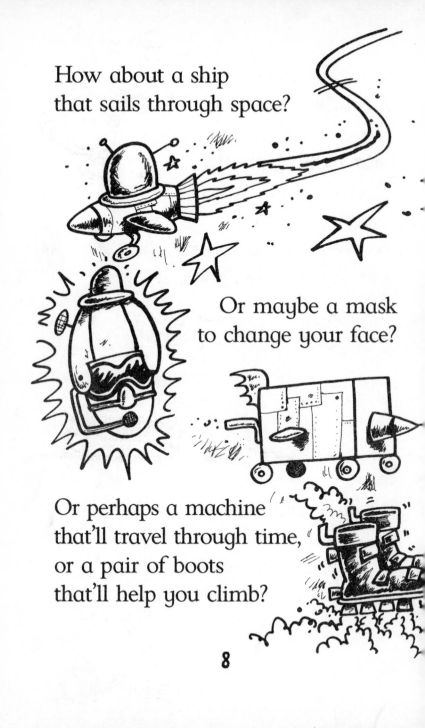

Or maybe a mask
to change your face?

Or perhaps a machine
that'll travel through time,
or a pair of boots
that'll help you climb?

8

Or a flying bike
from bits of clocks,
or a crazy contraption
for making chocs?"

"Nah!" said Frank,
"That ain't no fun.
That's all kids' stuff.
It's all been done!

9

So what'll I do
to drop their jaws
and bring me all
their loud applause?"

"I wonder if,"
he mused, "I can
put together
my very own man.
And make him walk
and come alive,
teach him to talk
and juggle and jive.

10

No one's managed
that before.
So that's the thing
I'll try, for sure!"
So he got two guys
with a horse and cart,
and he gave them a picture
of each part.

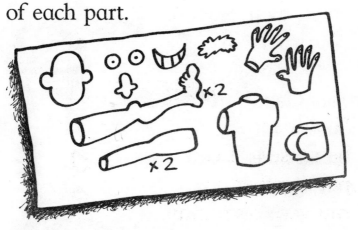

He sent them out
to find each bit,
then he worked out how
to make them fit.

Legs connected
up to feet.
Stitch them firmly,
nice and neat.

Other ends
join up to torso.
Stitch them tightly,
even more so.

Torso leads off
onto arm.
Some Superglue
will do no harm.

Shoulders need
a solid neck.
Stitch and sew
and trim and check.

And a body might
as well be dead,
unless it's got
a great big head.

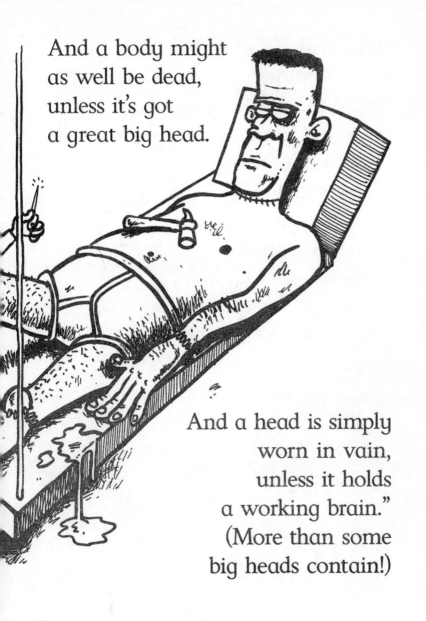

And a head is simply
worn in vain,
unless it holds
a working brain."
(More than some
big heads contain!)

13

But Frank didn't know
that the monster's brain
had come from a guy
who died insane.
"Insane?" you ask.
"And is that bad?"
Why, yes. It means:
completely mad.

Imagine a guy
three metres tall,
who's absolutely
up the wall!
What will happen?
Where will it end,
when a monster goes
right round the bend?

14

When Frank had got
his monster ready,
he laid him down
to keep him steady.
He strapped him firmly
onto the bed
and wound a wire
round his head.

Then he waited for
the next big storm
to wake him up
and make him warm.

And at the first
great thunderclap,
the monster stirred
and broke a strap.
The monster stretched
and gave a yawn.
"At last!" cried Frank.
"My son is born."

Then, at the very
next big crash,
the wire went *FIZZ!*
and the eyes went *FLASH!*

And the big guy rose
with an angry roar
and knocked Frank flat
upon the floor.

Said Frank, "But son,
it's me, your dad."
Said the monster, "Man,
don't make me mad.
You may think you've
invented me,
but now I'm here
I wanna be free!"

And he stomped out into
the wind and rain,
saying, "Don't expect me
back again."

But the guy was big
and much too strong.
And furthermore,
he didn't half pong!
He was sewn together
from dug-up bits,
so he scared most people
out of their wits!

He crashed around
and knocked things down,
and soon he'd smashed up
half the town.

He broke all the windows
and crushed the cars.
He cleaned out all
the pizza bars!
So the people said
he'd have to go,
though no one dared
to tell him so.

But in the end
they formed a band,
and hunted him
across the land.
And if he stopped
and stomped his boot,
they pelted him
with rotten fruit.

And if he tried
to rage and roar,
they called him names
and threw some more.

But just as this
was getting boring,
they heard a helicopter
roaring.
Out leaned a man
with a big cigar,
saying, "Come with me.
I'll make you a star."

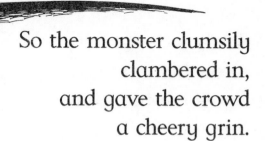

So the monster clumsily
clambered in,
and gave the crowd
a cheery grin.

"Hey, folks,
this helicopter's good.
Whoopee! I'm off
to Hollywood.
I guess I'll be
the only star
with a bolt in the neck
and a stitched-up scar!

Sorry to leave you.
Don't be annoyed.
You'll see me soon
on celluloid."

And before too long
their local star
could be seen at the city
cinema.

Then Doctor Frank
sang out with joy,
"Just look at that, folks.
That's my boy!"

And yes, you guessed,
that angry crowd,
when they saw this,
they all felt proud.
They bragged as they stood
in the box-office line,
pointing up
to the bright-lit sign.

"Hey, look! That's Frankie's son,
our friend!"
There's people for you.
That's THE END.

**A** long time ago
near the banks of the Nile
(home of the hungry
croc-o-dile)